First Generation

Eastern & North Eastern Region Diesels

In Colour

David Dunn

Copyright Book Law Publications – First published in the United Kingdom in 2018

ISBN 978-1-909625-85-3

Printed and bound by The Amadeus Press, Cleckheaton, West Yorkshire

Published by Book Law Publications, 382 Carlton Hill, Nottingham, NG4 1JA

INTRODUCTION

The title of this album is correct for the content herein. The fact that the Eastern Region swallowed up the North Eastern Region in 1966 does not really have a bearing even though some of the images are post 66' in order to tell the story of the motive power situation on the regions illustrated and perhaps BR in general. We have tried to follow a geographical route from north to south and in doing so have also moved from east to west so that we have covered as much ground as possible. Some locations get more than one image in order to show off their features from different aspects and angles although each time we have moved just around the corner or to the opposite side of a junction. All in all the mix is, in our estimation, a good variety of stations, junctions, industrial installations, motive power depots, bridges, and events.

Like the album covering the 1st Generation diesels in Scotland, the bulk of the illustrations presented here were captured on film by the late John Boyes who found some extraordinary places to perch himself and his camera in order to get that special image. In order to have access to John's extensive portfolio we must thank the Trustees of the Armstrong Railway Photographic Trust (ARPT) for giving us permission to reproduce them here for your delectation. We must also thank Jim Sedgwick for the use of Richard Holland slides and the other contributors who's images have helped to enhance this album – thank you Gentlemen.

David Dunn, Cramlington, 2018.

(Cover) See Page 25.

(Rear Cover top) See Page 83.

(Rear Cover bottom) See Page 84.

(Title page) Negotiating that fabulous diamond crossing, Brush Type 4 D1913 heads north from a quiet Newcastle (Central), with the afternoon York-Edinburgh parcels (3S46), on Friday 30th June 1967. The conductor rails of the erstwhile Tyneside electric system – serving platforms 1 to 6 – have taken on light rust since the last electric trains ran just thirteen days beforehand on Saturday 17th June. Newcastle's skyline was changing with more high-rise building replacing the terraced properties. *John Boyes (ARPT).*

TWEEDMOUTH & SOUTH TO TYNESIDE

When Gateshead got a batch of new Brush Type 4s from Crewe during April and May 1964 - D1574 to D1582 - 52A shed ran them in on easy workings such as stopping passenger trains and one regular turn was the 0730 Berwick to Newcastle stopper. D1578 had made its way north on Friday 15th May 1964, stabling overnight at Tweedmouth engine shed. Next morning we see the fortnight-old diesel at Tweedmouth on that 0730 'stopper' waiting for the 'right-away' from the station staff. Note that a certain amount of road dirt has already begun to cover the underframe and body of the Brush which was released from Crewe on the 2nd May, two weeks previously. Savour that fairly clean paintwork because there aren't too many of those in here! Tweedmouth station no longer exists. Opened for business on 29th March 1847 the establishment closed just a month after this image was recorded and from there on the 0730 'stopper' no longer called. *John Boyes (ARPT).*

After fourteen miles, we arrive at Belford; this undated view of the station reveals 'Peak' D175 running south with an unidentified Up afternoon express at the height of summer in Northumberland. The layout of the station is typical NER with the main offices on the Down side, waiting shed on the Up side, and with a grandiose goods shed on the east side. Opened in 1847, the station was closed on 29th January 1968. The NER footbridge has been painted in the regional grey but steam locomotives keep leaving reminders of their presence. D175 was one of the Gateshead fleet of what was to become Class 46 under the TOPS scheme (46038) and was Derby built from August 1962; its external condition would have us believe this image was captured in 1963. *John Boyes (ARPT).*

An Up express pauses at Alnmouth on the evening of Saturday 7th May 1966. The motive power is a rather grotty (we did warn you) EE Type 4, D271 from York which certainly hadn't been cleaned since its transfer from Gateshead earlier in the year. On the left, in the Alnwick line platform is Peppercorn K1 No.62021 which had brought in the train from the Alnwick branch earlier. The engine shed stands on the extreme left and was providing the engines for the branch workings and the stopping trains to Newcastle which were still steam hauled. *John Boyes (ARPT)*.

Haymarket 'Deltic' D9013 THE BLACK WATCH with 1A16 the Down *FLYING SCOTSMAN* on Saturday 19th March 1966 passing one of the coastal views on offer to passengers near Alnmouth. Note the 'flying thistle' headboard; now what happened to those few examples, and how many were produced? *John Boyes (ARPT)*.

An unusual choice of motive power for a rail tour but the North East Rail-tour of Sunday 29th September 1963 had this Robert Stephenson & Hawthorn built Drewry 204 h.p. 0-6-0 diesel-mechanical at the front/back of the train. This compiler knows little of the working or the actual tour, indeed who organised it! However, our little diesel, D2326, was a resident of Percy Main which would make sense on its employment. Just over two years old, the six-coupled DM started life at Tyne Dock shed on 2nd June 1961 but transferred north of the Tyne on 8th June 1963. When Percy Main closed on 27th February 1966, D2326 and her sisters were taken in by Gateshead depot which then had one of the largest allocations of the Drewry type 0-6-0DM in the country. It wasn't to last however and BR got rid of many of the class (TOPS 04) to industry or scrap. After withdrawal on 20th August 1968 D2326 ended up with the NCB at Manvers Main Colliery. *R.F.Payne (ARPT).*

In contrast to D2326 at Blyth, we present one of the BR-built examples (Doncaster, August 1959) which became TOPS Class 03. With its pre-TOPS number D2066 but in corporate blue, with yellow buffer beams, chevron stripes, and the BR double-arrow symbol, this 0-6-0DM was recently ex-works but we have no date for this image which was captured at the western end of Newcastle (Central) station. It would be some years before the electrification warning plates had any meaning on this section of the ECML. *Chris Campbell.*

With the last of its twelve vehicle load just leaving Manors station in their wake, Haymarket based ‘Deltic’ D9021 ARGYLL AND SUTHERLAND HIGHLANDER brings the Up *FLYING SCOTSMAN* into Central station during the late morning of Friday 30th June 1967. Note the kink in the track which was to facilitate the building of the Newcastle Central Motorway. *John Boyes (ARPT)*.

One of Gateshead's 'Peak' fleet sets out from Newcastle to Edinburgh with a train from Bristol on 30th June 1967. The blue paint of BR's corporate image is slowly being applied to the main-line passenger locomotives as witness this prospective future Class 46. In the background 'Deltic' D9014 THE DUKE OF WELLINGTON'S REGIMENT has just arrived with an express from King's Cross. *John Boyes (ARPT).*

(left) Appearing to be virtually brand-new! 'Deltic' D9020 NIMBUS stands with the northbound service of *THE FLYING SCOTSMAN* in platform 8 at Central station on Monday 18th June 1962. This was no ordinary working; today was the centenary run of this iconic train (in 1862 it was timetabled as the 'Special Scotch Express' departing King's Cross at 10 o'clock in the morning). D9020 was already four months old and the staff at Finsbury Park depot had done a good job in preparing the Co-Co for this job.

Ian W. Coulson (ARPT).

(below) D9003 MELD has a Down express at Newcastle (Central) in August 1968. By now the BR corporate blue had started to appear on the 'Deltics' and every other locomotive passing through works for major overhauls. The full yellow ends really stood out against the blue livery as though the two were made for each other. Note also the two double arrow symbols and twin fleet numbers carried by the big diesel. This Finsbury Park based example was beginning to look somewhat jaded with road dirt climbing up the body side; standards were slipping and even depots like 34G began to copy the likes of Gateshead for instance.

Chris Campbell.

Crew change! Finsbury Park based D9018 BALLYMOSS shines in the early afternoon sun at the western end of Central station on a glorious Saturday 10th November 1962. The Up express is 1A35 – the 1035 Glasgow (Queen Street) – London (King's Cross). No doubt lunch is being served in the dining car! *John Boyes (ARPT)*.

They weren't always dirty! Gateshead's BR Sulzer Type 4 D176 starts away from Central with a southbound afternoon express in August 1968. *Chris Campbell.*

In complete contrast! Although the skyline of Newcastle stands out on the north end of the King Edward Bridge, the two-tone green Brush Type 4 heading this seven-vehicle working is virtually anonymous under its coating of filth. However, John Boyes did make a note of D1916's number when it was heading what appears to be a summer afternoon train on an unknown date circa 1965? *John Boyes (ARPT).*

Haymarket's D9004 QUEEN'S OWN HIGHLANDER had charge of the 1100 Edinburgh–London train on Sunday 21st March 1965 and negotiating the curve off the King Edward Bridge, the 'Deltic' is winding up for another high-speed run after its Newcastle stop. *John Boyes (ARPT).*

Before we leave Tyneside a quick visit to Gateshead Traction maintenance Depot would not go amiss. Locally-built D2321 (RSH Darlington 1961) stands in the evening sun at 52A on a date to be determined. The immediate background is formed by another RSH product, the slightly younger EE Type 3 D6827. Both locomotives are in the time-honoured Gateshead livery of layered filth which was becoming popular all over BR. The recently painted bufferbeam on the Drewry must have been something to do with safety because the rear end has also been so treated. As already mentioned, many of these contractor-built 0-6-0DM had a short BR life but many went into industry to put in some useful time. D2321 was one of the unlucky examples and after withdrawal in July 1968 it was purchased by a firm on Teesside, for scrap! *Chris Campbell.*

Besides its portion of the 'Deltic' fleet, Gateshead had many other main-line diesel locomotives allocated and one of the most memorable classes were the BR-built Sulzer Type 4s which became Class 46 under TOPS. Still wearing its 'D' this is D149 on the shed yard on 6th October 1970 with sister 148 behind and EE Type 4 – still green – 252 on the left. All of Class 46 were eventually allocated to Gateshead except for eight of them which ended their days at Plymouth Laira where they balanced the motive power requirements on the cross-country, inter-regional, passenger workings between Tyneside and the West Country. Amongst the heaviest of all BR's diesel locomotives, these 2,500 h.p. monsters were among the quietest on the rails. Ten years after this image was captured on film D149 alias 46012 was in the midst of scrap at Swindon awaiting its fate! *Ian Falcus.*

Whistling its way across the junction whilst hauling a rather mixed freight, English Electric Type 3 D6782 heads east through Pelaw on Saturday 7th September 1968. The station on the left, which by now consisted an unmanned island platform, dated from November 1896 and was built on the site of the original 1839 station which was re-sited in the 1850s to a spot just behind the photographer but which had to be relocated again when the junctions were established. Pelaw BR station closed on Bonfire Night 1979 but was re-opened as a Tyne & Wear establishment in September 1985. *John Boyes (ARPT).*

A Tyne Dock-Consett iron-ore working (8K06) appears to be strolling up the incline near Stanley on 11th August 1966. At the head is BR Sulzer Type 2 D5182 with EE Type 4 D251 banking. It will be noted that the train consists of nine hoppers and a brake van whereas in steam days before the 9Fs were transferred in to work these trains the usual load was eight hoppers and a brake for the O1s and Q7s. The brake van was discarded eventually and the banker was only required when a single diesel worked the train as here. Double-headed Type 2s became the norm until March 1974 when the Tyne Dock operation was wound-up and ore was brought from Middlesbrough in different hoppers hauled by different motive power. But nothing lasts forever – industrial Britain especially – and even those workings ceased in 1980 as the steelworks at Consett were shut down and another chunk of British history was seemingly discarded as scrap! *Dave Tyreman (ARPT).*

COUNTY DURHAM

Hauling a train of loaded coal hoppers towards Hartlepool, Thornaby based EE Type 3 D6770 enters the long-closed (9th June 1952) Hesleden station precincts on the Saturday afternoon of 14th January 1967. The low winter sun is managing to highlight all the relevant areas for the photographer but this image is itself highlighting the dereliction, destruction and general untidiness of the industry which once dominated this part of Britain put was by now clinging on to the last vestiges of life. In the background the twin headgear of the closed Castle Eden Colliery stands out in that red-lead finish so popular with such installations. The cutting for the rail connection to the mine has been filled-in and everything else has been left to rot. *John Boyes (ARPT).*

The train workings in County Durham which served the coal industry had some weird paths in order to get both full and empty hoppers to where they were required. This empty train from Tees yard to Hawthorne is heading west through the derelict Hesleden station on 16th March 1967 with an unidentified BR Sulzer Type 2, complete with brake tender (DBT). The island-platform station dated from circa 1851 but was rebuilt and renamed – from Castle Eden Colliery – in 1891. Note the yellow warning panel on the Sulzer is actually orange. We'll see more of those panels later. *John Boyes (ARPT)*.

Heading south with a parcels train, EE Type 4 D247 runs beneath the signal box at Penshaw North Junction on 16th April 1967. This once busy junction is long gone, it's various routes, colliery lines, flyovers and junctions just a memory for those who remember the hustle and bustle of freight after freight. *John Boyes (ARPT)*.

A half-decent Brush Type 4, D1588, runs south with Up cement empties from Dunbar to London on the morning of Thursday 25th August 1966. The location is Plawsworth viaduct between Chester-le-Street and Durham, approximately ten miles south of Newcastle (Central). The Up line is in the ascent here so some of those 2,750 units of horsepower locked up inside that Brush would be needed for the climb. The full bloom of the surrounding foliage makes for a magical image. *John Boyes (ARPT)*.

A diverted Up express runs through Bishop Auckland East junction on 20th August 1967. It is a Sunday when most of these diversions take place and those in the know could get to some of the more obscure locations to catch an event such as this as D1500 takes the curve through the somewhat austere and meagre station; of course there would be more diverted expresses so a 'pick and mix' of suitable places was the order of the day. What's more, the weather was perfect. Some enthusiasts however liked to ride the trains covering mileage not often trod by passenger trains. Bishop Auckland is still served by train but not on this scale; diversions off the ECML are no longer possible and just a single line passes through the town heading west to nowhere in particular. *John Boyes (ARPT)*.

Another Finsbury Park Brush – D1516 – heads an Up express through Bishop Auckland East junction on a different Sunday a fortnight later on 3rd September 1967 – note the weather again! The train is our old friend 1A31, the 0900 Edinburgh (Waverley) to London (King's Cross) with an enthusiastic Secondman (probably the Driver letting his Secondman get some time in at the controls of the big diesel) peering out of the window. Even here the track gang is busy but just look at that magnificent signal gantry which is already being made semi-redundant. *John Boyes (ARPT)*.

A parting shot of Bishop Auckland and its townscape; at the other end of community now with an unidentified EE Type 3 and a brake van heading through North junction towards Toronto, and eventually Brancepeth Colliery. Sunday 8th March 1968. This is the route the diverted ECML expresses would have used. *John Boyes (ARPT)*.

(*above*) Once the diverted Up ECML expresses had left Bishop Auckland behind, they had to negotiate a tunnel which emerged near Shildon. Here on 10th December 1967 another diverted Up express (1A17) – headed by Brush D1992 – emerges from that tunnel into bright winter sunshine and some fresh overnight snow. *R.Goad (ARPT)*.

(*below*) A superb winter view at Relly Mill on Sunday 31st January 1965! 'Deltic' D9007 PINZA was temporarily shattering the peaceful scene whilst heading an Up express. *John Boyes (ARPT)*.

Back on the route of the Tyne Dock-Consett iron-ore workings, we have this undated view of a pair of BR Sulzer Type 2s creating a bit of exhaust whilst hauling a load up to Consett. These diesels certainly were the charges of 52A, the filth on their bodywork only relieved by the clean yellow warning panel. Note the rust stain on the permanent way; that stain existed all the way from Tyne Dock Bottom to Consett steelworks. *I.S.Carr (ARPT).*

(left) An undated view of the departure sidings at Silksworth Colliery: A pair of BR-built 0-6-0DM shunters ready to run a loaded coal train down to Ryhope. Sunderland depot supplied the motive power for these workings for which they adapted pairs of these BR-built Drewry shunters to work in tandem. *I.S. Carr (ARPT).*

(below) The twins at home in Sunderland; the electrical connections between the pair are evident. There were others likewise fitted. *Chris Campbell.*

D9003 MELD runs on the Leamside lines at Ferryhill on a glorious Mayday 1966 whilst working the 0900 Edinburgh (Waverley) to London (King's Cross). *John Boyes (ARPT)*.

Just a fortnight beforehand winter tried to make a comeback but the crew of Brush 4 D1582 would hardly notice in their cab as the Type 4 runs on the main line through Ferryhill cutting with a very-mixed Up goods on 15th April 1966. *John Boyes (ARPT)*.

A different aspect of the cutting at Ferryhill from the No.1 signal box reveals an unidentified 'Deltic' screaming through with a Glasgow (Queen Street)-London (Kings Cross) express on 23rd April 1963. *John Boyes (ARPT).*

An as yet to be named D9002 has charge of the 1200 London (King's Cross)–Glasgow (Queen Street) as it passes the island platforms at Ferryhill circa 1962. This was a Gateshead 'Deltic' and it appears to be immaculate! On the right are the remains of Ferryhill engine shed which had closed in November 1938 but which had only recently been demolished. During World War II the shed had been utilised to store preserved locomotives from York railway museum. BR also found the shed and yard useful, for storing withdrawn locomotives prior to their acceptance into Darlington shops. *John Boyes (ARPT).*

Now here is a rarity! Still unnamed D9010 stops for a signal at Ferryhill whilst heading an Up express. We have no date but we do know the 'Deltic' received its THE KING'S OWN SCOTTISH BORDERER name in May 1965 so this image could have been recorded during the previous winter, or the one before that!? What is interesting about this picture is the external condition of D9010. It was a Haymarket engine and they always looked after their charges; even the yellow warning panel is rather filthy! Was there an industrial dispute taking place? Oh yes, the train was being diverted; the perils of travelling on a Sunday! *John Boyes (ARPT)*.

Away from the ECML and back onto one of the myriad of secondary routes serving the collieries in the hinterland of County Durham; the date is unrecorded but it was winter and the locomotive has an all yellow front – 1967. More to the point, the EE Type 3, D6756, and her faithful brake tender have a heavy coal train in check on a seemingly descending gradient. If it's of any help, the train has just cleared a junction where the signal box stood between the two routes; ideas on a postcard please..... *John Boyes (ARPT)*.

(*above*) Returning to the ECML at Coxhoe junction, just north of Ferryhill, we have a meet, of sorts, with D9017 THE DURHAM LIGHT INFANTRY heading the Up working of the *QUEEN OF SCOTS* beneath the flyover just as Ivatt Class 4 No.43129 is stopped with *THE SOUTH DURHAM LIMITED* on 23rd May 1964. The stock of one train is made up of Pullman vehicles hauled by a filthy diesel whereas the other named train comprises half a dozen draughty brake vans, with dangerous open verandas, hauled by an immaculately turned-out steam locomotive. There is some irony in there somewhere! The branch joining the main line beneath the bridge was a colliery line from Coxhoe, go a little further south and another line – this time from Hartlepool – joins the main line; it is that line which takes us back east for a little interlude by the coast. *John Boyes (ARPT).*

(*below*) And so to the seaside where this particular Vulcan Foundry-built Drewry 0-6-0DM – D2205 – is worth a special mention because it spent most of its working life allocated to West Hartlepool engine shed (51C) from being put into traffic in March 1953 as No.11106. Renumbered in January 1959, the little DM was to be given those tiger-stripe ends with green livery; it also got a yellow buffer beam note! When 51C was closed to steam and down-graded to a stabling point status from 2nd September 1967, the 0-6-0DM was transferred to Thornaby for maintenance purposes but it still worked in West Hartlepool as here at Newburn Junction on 4th September 1967 in charge of a transfer goods. Somebody else must have liked D2205 because after being withdrawn in July 1969 it was purchased for preservation on a line far, far away from Hartlepool. *John Boyes (ARPT).*

WEST HARTLEPOOL

Making its way through Hartlepool via the scenic route, EE Type 4 D254 has charge of a rather mixed bag of coaching stock passing through Church Street on 14th June 1967. Amongst the variety are two Kitchen Cars, SR parcels vans, GUVs, a Royal Mail sorting coach, and a blue spot Fish van. Goodness knows what the destination of this train was but York wouldn't be crossed off the list of possibilities just yet. *John Boyes (ARPT).*

Another EE Type 4 on another coaching stock movement or is this a parcels train? D257 runs through Newburn Junction on 5th July 1967. Steam traction is winding down on the Eastern Region (the NE Region having amalgamated with the ER in 1966) and West Hartlepool engine shed on the left has become one of the last bastions of steam in the north-east. The dilapidated buildings of 51C are clearly ready for demolition even the recently added diesel repair shop looks clapped-out. *John Boyes (ARPT).*

(*above*) From the final batch of Type 1s built by English Electric came D8310 and D8312 which with 'newness' still oozing from their bodyworks, were running through Newburn Junction during the late afternoon of Thursday 10th August 1967 en route to Thornaby depot. The pair of Bo-Bos were delivered to BR on 28th April 1967 in this blue livery complete with double-arrow symbols and with the 'D' prefix. Thornaby received D8310 to D8315 but less than a year later on 23rd March 1968 they all transferred to Dairycoates; we will see one of them later in Hull! *John Boyes (ARPT)*.

(*below*) For our last image of West Hartlepool, let's finish off with a 'Deltic' in town: D9002 – looking a bit scruffy – passes Church Street on Thursday 8th June 1967 with a southbound passenger working. Now when is that weed killing train due? *John Boyes (ARPT)*.

DURHAM

We've moved inland to Durham now to continue our southward journey along the ECML axis for a while. Inevitably 'Deltics' are going to show up from all sides: D9012 CREPELLO thunders through the station with an Up express on 20th April 1964. There will be no requirement for a 'banker' with this train. *John Boyes (ARPT)*.

On the same day this Class 4 Up goods might need a banker but methinks the unidentified EE Type 4 has got its train nicely wound up for the gradient ahead. The layout of Durham station is evident in this view which shows a DMU in the Up bay platform. *John Boyes (ARPT)*.

An unidentified EE Type 4 (yes they were popular around here) drifts past Durham North box ready to run through the station on the Up fast with a short southbound freight on the 8th March 1964. The open ground on the Down side of the main line, opposite the signal box, was once occupied by Durham engine shed, a small two-road building which had a turntable to the rear. A sub shed to Sunderland, the establishment closed in December 1958 after being home to at least two A8 Pacific tanks for many years. *John Boyes (ARPT).*

Doing what it says on the box, D9006 comes off the viaduct and accelerates ready for the run through Durham station with the Down *FLYING SCOTSMAN* on 20th April 1964. *John Boyes (ARPT).*

Just to the south of Durham viaduct two schoolboys observe EE Type 4 D252 getting to grips with an Up parcels train on a glorious 20th August 1967. *John Boyes (ARPT)*.

(*above*) EE Type 4 D283 brings a noisy train of what appears to be scrap through the Up platform at Durham on 20th April 1964. These 2,000 h.p. monsters had enjoyed a short period working the prestige express passenger trains on the ECML but now they were relegated to work duties such as this. It turns out that they were eminently suited to goods, parcels, passenger or in fact any working. They were impressive locomotives and perhaps under-powered for their bulk but they nevertheless made you take notice whenever they ran through a station at high speed. *John Boyes (ARPT)*.

(*below*) 'And the same to you chief!' might have been the reply to the Platform Inspector from the Driver if he could have been heard! D9019 makes the usual 'Deltic' departure from Durham with a London-bound express on a chilly 8th March 1964. *John Boyes (ARPT)*.

DARLINGTON

Diesel-Steam combinations were never that common even in the early years of dieselisation so this gem from circa winter 1961 at Darlington is worth inclusion. The EE Type 4 is D357 from Haymarket and was delivered to BR on the penultimate day of August 1961. Why the big diesel is being attached to a parcels train headed by B1 No.61304 is something of a mystery in that 64B main-line diesels were not that common around these parts. A list of reasons for its attendance here could be easily drawn up but we do not have that much space. The presence of the B1 is easily explained in that it was allocated to 51A! *K.H.Cockerill (ARPT).*

Gateshead 'Peak' D179 winds its ten-vehicle train out of Bank Top station and onto the Up fast ready for some fast running over the racetrack to York on 15th June 1964. 52A hasn't let us down regarding reputation; even the route indication box and warning panel haven't been cleaned! *John Boyes (ARPT).*

Some pictures can make you feel cold by looking at them; this image is one of those! The date is 14th November 1968 and the combination of fog and very low air temperatures has created a blanket of frost over D9017 and its (1A21) Up express rolling stock. Hopefully it was warmer inside both but methinks otherwise. *John Boyes (ARPT).*

(*above*) The locomotive works at Darlington had been responsible for building hundreds of locomotives over the decades since it was opened by the North Eastern Railway. BR continued building steam locomotives there and then diesels came onto the scene, firstly in the shape of the 350 h.p. 0-6-0DE shunters and later these BR Sulzer Type 2s of which five are in various stages of construction on 2nd March 1964. None are recorded by the cameraman but we do know that twenty – D7578 to D7597 – were completed between November 1963 and August 1964, the last locomotives constructed at BR's Darlington North Road workshops. *R.Goad (ARPT).*

(*below*) Repair work went on at the North Road shops until the very end. On 1st July 1964 a couple of 'Peaks' are in works whilst an accident damaged Gateshead-based EE Type 3 D6785 gets its front-end straightened out! *R.Goad (ARPT).*

D243 runs on the Up fast in June 1972 with the diesel multiple unit maintenance depot on the right, and the remains of the former steam locomotive depot (51A), actually out of sight, on the left. The station lies ahead but the big EE Type 4 will by-pass the platforms and stay on the main line heading south. Darlington it appears is as busy as ever with plenty going on. *Sam Woods*.

International Rescue Darlington branch! It's the kind of event BR didn't like to have publicised but it was becoming all too prevalent as standards dropped (across the board) and equipment was wearing out. However, it wasn't too often the EE Type 4 was in trouble but D239 working a Down fitted freight had come unstuck somewhere south of Darlington on 3rd August 1968. The cavalry, in the shape of station pilot D2155 recently ex-works and looking very smart, turned up and hauled the Type 4 and its train back off the main line and into a place of convenience. D239 was from Gateshead's fleet so it was unusual to see one of theirs requiring assistance but more to the point, the big diesel was clean! *R.Holland.*

Going back in time to the days when the steam Motive Power Depot was still operational and being a nuisance to local households on washing day. Sulzer Type 2 D5153 heads south with a loaded coal train; the coal looks like the kind of stuff power station furnaces could devour. The aforementioned MPD is on the horizon, its coaling plant and water tower being local landmarks. Note the prefabs on the right, still occupied; most people I know who lived in those 'temporary' houses thought they were superb and were sorry to leave them for more 'permanent' homes. The date: 15th June 1964. *John Boyes (ARPT).*

TEES SIDE

This location could be regarded as the southern edge of West Hartlepool or the northern edge of Tees Side. We've chosen the later simply because it brings us nicely into a sequence of images depicting the industrial sprawl built up around the River Tees and now labelled Tees Side. Okay, you've guessed it – Seaton Carew where the steel plants of Hartlepool were left behind and a little fresh air was available for the few miles south to Billingham, Stockton, Redcar, Thornaby and Middlesbrough which together became Tees Side in April 1968. The locomotive is D5155, working a West Hartlepool–Tees yard goods on 15th May 1965. *John Boyes (ARPT)*.

Skipping over Billingham for the time being we get to Stockton. Is this a Newcastle–Liverpool express or one of the East Coast workings via Sunderland and Stockton? Whatever the train, the locomotive is distinctive in being a Gateshead 'Peak' – D175 apparently – which is just getting its train on the move again after a stop in Stockton. This junction is Bishopton Lane, according to the signal box name but note those dwelling houses on the right. It's like the American mid-west without all the bells ringing! *John Boyes (ARPT)*.

Primrose Hill, Stockton, aka the Gas Works, 13th June 1965 with Gateshead EE Type 4 D256 contradicting the wall of abuse suffered by the authorities at 52A regarding locomotive cleaning. The train is the 1710 Newcastle (Central) to Liverpool (Lime Street) which was one of the more adventurous 'expresses' running between the two cities. The combination of routes used by these Newcastle-Liverpool trains was quite interesting. First of all there was the station situation at Liverpool; was it Lime Street or Central? That depended on the historical origin of the working – LNWR or LYR. The routes varied in that you could travel along the ECML Newcastle to York, on to Leeds, over the Standedge route via Huddersfield to Manchester (Exchange), then via Earlstown to Lime Street. But the Newcastle to Leeds section could go thus: Newcastle (Central), to Sunderland via Felling, Hartlepool, Stockton, Northallerton, Ripon, Harrogate, Leeds, Halifax, Summit tunnel, Rochdale, Manchester (Victoria), Wigan (Wallgate), Liverpool (Central); or a permutation of any parts of the above. If you were in a hurry you didn't board the train illustrated but if you were an enthusiast you made time and got this working around the houses and all the scenic treats County Durham and Yorkshire had on offer. Not having the relevant timetable to hand I'm not sure of the ETA of this train but there wouldn't be much daylight left on arrival in Liverpool. It could however be a diversion too! Note the ten-coach formation complete with Kitchen car. 'Those were the days!' *John Boyes (ARPT)*.

(*above*) Peppercorn K1 No.62044 stops for water (one of the problems associated with steam locomotives) beside the train shed at Stockton station on the evening of Wednesday 19th April 1967. Alongside EE Type 3 D6770 and its DBT are on a train of iron ore empties which has just been given the signal to proceed further. *John Boyes (ARPT)*.

(*below*) Stratford based Brush D1779 departs Stockton freightliner terminal on Thursday 25th July 1968 with the 2030hrs working to Stratford. *John Boyes (ARPT)*.

(*above*) To do Tees Side in strict rotational and geographical order is somewhat difficult with every nook and cranny vying for attention first. We've done Stockton and now it's off to Billingham where straight away we come across a little puzzle. This is Billingham station on 11th April 1965 with an EE Type 3 working a passenger train wrong-line! The other end – the 'proper' end – has a 'Peak' attached as the train engine and the unidentified Type 3 was coupled simply to haul the ensemble around the Beck branch which was both single-line and quite torturous. We'll be seeing a few more of these diversions over the following pages. Now, note the level of the front room windows on the station house on the right. The station and the house date from the 1840s when platforms were much lower, hence the series of level changes over the years. This station was replaced by a modern establishment in November 1966 located some three-quarters of a mile to the east. *John Boyes (ARPT)*.

(*below*) D1579, one of Gateshead's trusted Brush Type 4s runs through the open countryside near Billingham with a Newcastle to Lincoln express on Monday 29th March 1965. *John Boyes (ARPT)*.

The view from the A19 Trunk road at Billingham shows the closed passenger station on 19th October 1967 and reveals the Royal Train (1X01) waiting at the station. D1985 is the designated train engine – one of Gateshead's lot – and a Thornaby Type 3 also suitably 'bulled-up' played both stand-by and other positions; there was even a bowler hat in the cab! The reason for the Royal visit was the official opening of the Billingham Forum by H.M. Queen and the Duke of Edinburgh; the public had been using the facility since the previous July. The Royal party were in Billingham for less than 60-minutes before they were back on their train. On that same day the Queen opened the new 'six-years-in-the-making' Tyne tunnel which linked the two sections of the A1 trunk road on either side of the river. *John Boyes (ARPT).*

This illustration shows the Queen arriving at Billingham on that occasion in October 1967; the Type 3 is bringing the train in rear-end first. We are assuming the train arrived from the ECML at Geneva curve Darlington, through Eaglescliffe, Stockton to the triangular junction at Roseworth where the Type 3 was then coupled. Of course the early locations may be completely wrong because the choice of routes was much better then, and the train may have spent the night somewhere secretive! Using the Beck branch would have saved a lot of messing about but! *John Boyes (ARPT).*

Just in case you forgot what winter looked like, what with all the excitement of the Royal visit, etc., we present a nice seasonal view of the main line in open country again as a Middlesbrough to Newcastle parcels passes through Billingham on Saturday 15th January 1966. The motive power was Type 2 D5102. *John Boyes (ARPT)*.

Illustrating another steam/diesel combination is 350 h.p. 0-6-0DE shunter D3672 from West Hartlepool hauling a ‘dead’ WD No.90230, also from West Hartlepool, away from Tees Side and through Billingham on the clear and crisp morning of Wednesday 9th November 1966. Although the details of this working are unknown, one assumption could have the diesel travelling from home to rescue the failed Austerity from a location on Tees Side, Thornaby engine shed being the favourite. As was usual with this class of steam locomotives, this example is totally filthy. However, the 2-8-0 was put back into working order by the fitters at 51C and it continued in employment for a couple more months at least. It was eventually condemned on 24th May 1967, some-time before steam was finally eliminated in this region of BR. Note that the shunter appears to be emulating its load but 51C were somewhat short of cleaners; D3672 moved on to Thornaby on 7th October 1967 and there they had a washing machine. *John Boyes (ARPT)*.

D6768 at Billingham with a train of returning Thrislington (near Ferryhill) Dolomite ore empties on the morning of 3rd September 1968. On the Up side a train of loaded coal hoppers has been left, as has the still smoking fire in the brake van. *John Boyes (ARPT).*

The 1145 Newcastle–Lincoln express leaving Billingham behind D1527 on 20th March 1965. *John Boyes (ARPT).*

(*above*) Passing through Billingham in November 1965 and en route to one of the Durham collieries equipped to load MGR wagons (HAAs), a train of new, air-braked, high capacity hopper wagons from Shildon wagon works sit comfortably behind Brush D1889. This wagon design and the infrastructure associated with MGR would revolutionise coal movements between pits and power stations, and other industries requiring large amounts of coal. *John Boyes (ARPT)*.

(*below*) No doubt bound for one of the industries located around Haverton Hill, EE Type 4 D367 and its DBT wait for rear-end assistance at Billingham with their train of coal hoppers on 1st February 1965. The WD 2-8-0 must be a West Hartlepool resident because Thornaby had got rid of its last examples in 1964. *John Boyes (ARPT)*.

BRC&W Type 2 D5370 heads through Billingham station on 18th September 1964 for Tees yard with a train from the nearby ICI plant. *John Boyes (ARPT)*.

Whilst working a diverted passenger train, our old friend from 52A, 'Peak' D175 slows at Haverton Hill South box so that the Secondman can take the staff from the Signal Bobby. The passengers, or at least those aware on this Sunday 11th April 1965 working, must have wondered where the train was actually going. Luckily for us our photographer knew all about the diversions and was on hand to record many of them. *John Boyes (ARPT)*.

A month later on Saturday 15th May 1965, at the same location, EE Type 4 D244 hauling a diverted Newcastle–Liverpool express swings across the points at Haverton Hill South. This image shows more of the surrounding industrial landscape. *John Boyes (ARPT).*

Passing through the North Tees C power station complex, Gateshead based Brush 4 D1988 has charge of the 1200 Philips Imperial Petroleum sidings to Bromsgrove tanks – 4Z20 – on Friday 23rd February 1968. *John Boyes (ARPT).*

The view from a very lofty position on the North Tees power station 24th February 1968: we are not quite sure where John Boyes was perched to capture this scene but it could have been the roof of the turbine hall, atop a chimney or even a cooling tower! Thankfully he remembered his camera and we have this landscape showing chemical plants and refineries in the distance to the north; below is the main line with a Type 2 and brake van in the frame whilst the power station's own sidings contain coal hoppers galore along with a steam locomotive, CEGB No.26, dragging full wagons through the unloading shed. No wonder Merry-Go-Round became popular. *John Boyes (ARPT).*

Steam hung on in this area of BR until September 1967 leaving the mantle of the final stronghold to be taken up by a handful of engine sheds in Lancashire. This view at Bowesfield on 7th December 1966 shows westbound WD Austerity 2-8-0, No.90309 and its brake van passing an equally filthy EE Type 3, D6777 working a Down goods. *John Boyes (ARPT)*.

Remember E2001? No! What about E1000? No! Well this is the locomotive which eventually became those two electric locomotives – 18100 – the Metropolitan-Vickers gas turbine. Built between 1948 and 1951 the MV gas turbine was the first British-built locomotive of its type. It went into testing and then road trials on the Western Region but by early November 1953 the WR basically discarded the locomotive and the gas turbine idea too, and so No.18100 was taken to Dukinfield. Having languished in the Manchester plants of Metro-Vicks for five years, the locomotive was hauled in early 1958 from Trafford Park to Bowesfield works in Stockton for conversion to an a.c. electric locomotive. Here on Sunday 12th October 1958, still as No.18100 note, the refurbished hulk with its electrical control gear installed along with a single pantograph on the roof is seen being taken to Manchester via Bowesfield Junction. The locomotive was renumbered E1000 on arrival in Manchester and the rest is history. The number of the WD 2-8-0 doing the honours was No.90377 from Thornaby. *R.F.Payne (ARPT)*.

Remember earlier we had that BR Sulzer Type 2 working empty hoppers through a derelict Hesleden station. The yellow warning panel was mainly orange! Well here is D5159 at Bowesfield on a Tees yard to Ferryhill goods on 10th December 1966. Look at the warning panel which is mainly orange with a yellow portion at the bottom. The Type 2 was one of Thornaby's charges so the experiment, if it was such, was conducted on 51L's fleet, or at least some of them. Does anyone know anything about the orange panels? If so we would like to hear from you via the usual channels. Thanks in anticipation! *John Boyes (ARPT).*

The docks are within a stone's throw of Type 3 D6755 and its DBT working a Down Tees yard to South Bank ore train through Guisborough junction, Middlesbrough on the warm evening of Monday 10th May 1965. When the British Steel Corporation was created, they invested a lot in infrastructure including equipping a new unloading wharf for ships bringing iron ore to Tees Side. High capacity bogie wagons were built to transport the ore to the blast furnaces and those same wagons were further utilised to run iron ore up to the BSC plant at Consett using EE type 3s from Thornaby. That decision sealed the fate of the Tyne Dock iron ore facility, and it's ageing fleet of wagons. *John Boyes (ARPT).*

Hauling a short train of tanks and with the setting sun in the Driver's eyes, D5163 approaches Guisborough junction with caution on 8th May 1967. A Merchantman' is partly in frame on the left but the identity of the vessel is unknown. *John Boyes (ARPT)*.

With industrial dereliction going through a seemingly endless cycle on Tees Side, this view of Middlesbrough's Oldtown has probably changed again since this image of 19th March 1965 was recorded. One of Thornaby's Birmingham Railway Carriage & Wagon Type 2s, D5378, was taking the Marsh branch goods in hand minus a brake van. From their arrival in 1962, these useful locomotives (D5370-D5378) did not spend a great deal of time at 51L, going south in January 1966 to the LM Region's Midlands area in a swap situation which brought an equal number of BR Sulzer Type 2s to Thornaby. In the background is the Newport Vertical Lift Bridge which was commissioned in 1934 and built by Dorman Long; with the machinery located on the actual lifting span, it brought the weight of that span up to 2,876 tonnes (note the metric stuff). Remember where you heard all these facts first! *John Boyes (ARPT)*.

After finishing its work further east, and now passing Whitehouse signal box, at Cargo Fleet, EE Type 3 D6770 runs 'light' back to Thornaby depot with a DBT and brake van on the evening of Wednesday 12th July 1967. *John Boyes (ARPT).*

Off for another day's graft, Thornaby's EE Type 3 D6777, DBT and brake van, run through South Bank, Middlesbrough on Tuesday 18th April 1967. On this side of the river it was mainly steel production and all its peripheral industries which blotted the landscape. On the north bank it was mainly chemicals which were dealt with. BR had a ready market on their doorstep although Thornaby depot was a product of BR bringing the motive power of four other local locomotive depots under one new roof in June 1958 – Haverton Hill, Middlesbrough, Newport, and Stockton. *John Boyes (ARPT).*

(*above*) Making its way to Middlesbrough docks from Dents Wharf with a train of export pipes bound for Saudi Arabia, BR 350 h.p. 0-6-0DE shunter D3150 passes through a leafy Hartburn junction on 3rd June 1965. This shunter started life at nearby Newport on 28th July 1955 but transferred to Darlington on 28th January of the following year. On 1st June 1958 it was sent to the new depot at Thornaby together with many of its siblings. However, just over ten years later it was withdrawn as 'Non-Standard' and surplus to BR's requirements. Although the BR 350 h.p. 0-6-0DE shunters have been extremely good servants, it was only the majority English Electric engine and EE traction motor fitted examples which were deemed standard. D3150 and her sisters D3137 to D3151 all had Blackstone engines and GEC traction motors and so became the black sheep of the 1000+ family. Of course there were others amongst the throng: D3152 to D3166 all had Blackstone engines but BTH traction motors: D3117 to D3126 had Crossley engines and Crompton Parkinson traction motors. There were literally a couple of hundred of these 'hybrids' and they all had an early demise. *John Boyes (ARPT)*.

(*below*) Same location, same day, different motive power, different train! Beyer, Peacock Clayton D8591 crosses the junction with a mixed freight. This was another class which had an early demise but it was nothing to do with standardisation and more to do with reliability problems. Ironically, on their introduction, this class was chosen by BR to become *the* Standard Type 1. However, circumstances and lots of other events changed that decision and the EE Type 1 became the Standard. *John Boyes (ARPT)*.

(*above*) The less salubrious part of Hartburn junction with another Blackstone 0-6-0DE shunter – D3141 – at the point of a Stockton North yard to Stockton Goods yard freight on 1st April 1965. *John Boyes (ARPT)*.

(*below*) D6763 and its DBT approaching Eaglescliffe station with a long train of iron-ore empties on Wednesday 16th August 1967. *John Boyes (ARPT)*.

D6819 positions itself and its train at Eaglescliffe station with the Viaduct Inspection Unit on Sunday morning 2nd July 1967. It looks as though Yarm viaduct could be getting a visit and what better day could be chosen for hanging in a cradle beneath a myriad of brick or stonework? *John Boyes (ARPT)*.

D5170 heads towards Darlington through Allens West on 20th May 1966. Note the single wagon load protected by two brake vans; I wonder what that rather unusual container contained (you don't hear that combination of words spoken too often)? The station here, indeed the signal box and the footbridge, all date from 1940 (the architecture gives us a clue) when the station was provided for munitions workers from the nearby naval depot at Carter Moor. The secrecy surrounding such installations carried on long after the end of hostilities and even the 1955 OS map shows nothing to indicate a station existed although the armaments depot is shown as a group of uniformly laid out buildings! The station was a Halt at first but that suffix was dropped when the public made use of the place from about 1971 apparently. It is still open. *John Boyes (ARPT)*.

(*above*) Yarm viaduct on the main line from Eaglescliffe to Northallerton which was favoured by goods trains from Tees Side to the south and vice versa. Spanning the River Tees where it is still fairly clean, the viaduct required two wide arches to span the waterway and its various architectural styles are evident from this aspect. Note the strengthening arches built within the existing arches. The Down goods train crossing the structure is headed by Thornaby's D376 and the date is 5th March 1966. *John Boyes (ARPT)*.

(*below*) This view of the viaduct gives it a more rustic look although that industrial brickwork is still showing on the right. D6766 is doing the honours on the main line with a Down lime train from Wensleydale to the iron works in Middlesbrough. *John Boyes (ARPT)*.

EE Type 4 D244 crosses the structure on 15th May 1966 with an Up express, probably one of the aforementioned Liverpool jobs. Below the locomotive and just above the centre pier in the river is a huge memorial to the main characters associated with this viaduct. The Engineers names are top, followed by the Superintendent, and finished off with the Contractors names. Yarm viaduct is now Grade II Listed and construction started in 1848 with the opening taking place in May 1852. These two skewed stone arches spanning the Tees are 65ft high and each span is 67ft wide; some 139,000 cubic feet of stone was used in their construction and other parts of the structure. The total cost of the build was £44,500 exactly which nowadays might get you a two-storey extension on your house, depending where you live! This part of the river used to be tidal until 1990 when a tidal barrier was built near Newport. *John Boyes (ARPT).*

Near the southern end of the viaduct on the morning of Saturday 16th March 1968, with D246 running a Down freight towards Tees yard. Note the new-build housing in the shadow of the structure. *John Boyes (ARPT).*

Two unidentified English Electric locomotives cross Yarm viaduct on 29th April 1966. Approaching is a Type 4 whilst running south is a Type 3. The full length on the structure is evident from this vantage point but the reason for the two brick arches being different from the rest is revealed by the historical subsidence, especially on this west parapet! The viaduct is still operational but the reason for the sinking is unknown to this compiler. It must have been a 'recent' problem because an image from 1898 shows the viaduct without any strengthening. The structure consists of forty-three arches and the total length is 2,280ft, or 760 yards, or 701 metres for those of you who have gone up-market. Besides the stone already mentioned, some seven and a half million bricks were used in the build. This end of the viaduct opened onto Yarm station which closed in January 1960. That station served the town of Yarm which was in the North Riding of Yorkshire whilst the station was in County Durham – the river was the county border. A new station serving Yarm opened in 1996 and that is just south of the viaduct. *John Boyes (ARPT).*

For our last look at Yarm we go into town where a brace of low-loader road vehicles have stopped in the high street on 9th July 1968 with unusual but nevertheless appropriate cargoes for this image. Sunters were the haulage contractors but the two locomotives were 0-6-0DMs D2306 and D2307. They were both ex-Thornaby and had been withdrawn during the previous February; the pair, en route to South Wales having been purchased by Duport Steel in Llanelly were part of batch containing three other 04s bought from Darlington depot. They enjoyed a dozen years of work before passing into preservation. *John Boyes (ARPT).*

NORTH & EAST YORKSHIRE

Wiske Moor water troughs north of Northallerton on the ECML were used not just be steam locomotives but also by diesels when they picked up water for their heating boilers. This 30th July 1963 image reveals that D1506, working the Up *ANGLO SCOTTISH CAR CARRIER*, did not pick up any water because of the season – BR had rules regarding train heating and summer was a definite No! These troughs continued in use long after steam had finished on the region because there was not enough rolling stock equipped with electric heating, nor locomotives able to supply that alternative heat until 1968. *John Boyes (ARPT)*.

D9017 THE DURHAM LIGHT INFANTRY was working an Up Anglo-Scottish express on 24th October 1964 when carriage heating was in full swing and the small capacity heating boiler supply tank required topping up at virtually every set of water troughs on the route. The 'Deltic' is certainly scooping a good amount here and you can now see one of the areas where the Secondman might earn his wages on these diesels. The whole idea of collecting water at speed had been explored thoroughly in steam days and there was apparently a magic figure of speed whereby the maximum amount of water could be picked-up at in the shortest possible time. However, I just can't bring that figure to mind; but D9017 had probably slowed down to dip the scoop! *John Boyes (ARPT)*.

(*above*) You can just hear those twin Deltic engines making that special noise as D9003 MELD heads south with the *ANGLO SCOTTISH CAR CARRIER* on Saturday 18th September 1965. This seasonal train will be getting towards its final working for the year by now – this might even be the last Up train – and any motorist wanting to get from the south-east of England to central Scotland will just have to drive during the winter months at least! The formation contained six car transporting vehicles and four for passengers. *John Boyes (ARPT)*.

(*below*) The 1966 season saw DP2 employed on various workings of the *ASCC* and here at Thirsk during the afternoon of 16th July 1966 the prototype speeds south with an Up service. Note the grounded coach body on the other side of the fence; I wonder what happened to that little gem? *John Boyes (ARPT)*.

Photographer John Boyes was amongst the list of accredited photographers whom British Railways trusted to attend incidents and record on film the outcome no matter how big or small. On 31st July 1967 John was working in Northallerton when he was asked to attend a collision at Codbeck on the main line south of Thirsk. What he didn't know until he arrived was the extent of the damage, what was involved, and the cost in both life and materials. As has already been well documented several times, the collision saw DP2, hauling a London-Edinburgh express, hitting at speed a derailed loaded wagon from a Cliffe-Uddingston cement train. This is DP2 which took the initial impact; miraculously neither the Driver or Secondman were injured whereas in the passenger vehicles behind the locomotive seven people lost their lives and dozens were injured. DP2 never recovered, the bodywork had suffered badly but its frame had been twisted by the impact and that fact sealed its fate. It was broken up in 1970. *John Boyes (ARPT)*.

(*below*) Moving west now, away from the carnage at Codbeck, we come to a line which was under threat when this image was actually recorded – 11th June 1964. The line was the former Leeds Northern Railway connection between Northallerton and Harrogate via Ripon and the structure which is the subject here is Ripon viaduct spanning the River Ure (and the A61 Trunk road) just south of Ripon station. Made of cast-iron, and appearing 'lightweight' when compared with the brick and stone bridges normally encountered, the structure was certainly strong and able to carry anything the railways could muster. Closed to passenger traffic in March 1967, the line south of Ripon was also closed to goods whereas the line to the north was not finally cut until 5th September 1969 when freight facilities at Ripon were withdrawn; the closure of the Ministry of Defence depot in October 1968 was another big loss to the line. The viaduct was demolished and much of the track bed, especially that in and around Ripon has been used for a by-pass road or built upon. The two images on this page have a connection in more ways than one; after the accident at Codbeck the ECML was essentially closed for three days and as an emergency measure the line south of Ripon had to be re-opened to serve as a diversionary route. Signal boxes and their batteries had to be re-instated, and signal men found to work the boxes. By 3rd August the ECML was restored fully and the Ripon line closed down once again. This viaduct was then demolished. The Deltic in view was D9011 THE ROYAL NORTHUMBERLAND FUSILIERS and the train was the Up *QUEEN OF SCOTS*. The concrete block foundations beneath each pier were provided by BR after heavy scouring threatened the structure in the 1950s. *John Boyes (ARPT)*.

(*above*) An undated view of Guisborough station in the 1960s: Thornaby Type 2 D5153 is heading a train of just two coaches. Approximately two-thirds of the passenger workings here comprised Middlesbrough–Scarborough services, with the balance made up of Whitby–Middlesbrough, and Middlesbrough–Guisborough services. Passenger traffic ceased in March 1964 and looking at this image, the passengers are somewhat thin-on-the-ground anyway and the whole thing looks somewhat depressing. The goods shed extension on the left was a BR innovation but it was short lived because the goods services were also withdrawn in 1964 at the end of the summer timetable. Guisborough's location at the end of a near–1,000 yard branch line was far from ideal and involved pushing and pulling trains to the junction with the main line. In LNER days a Sentinel railcar was employed on the Middlesbrough service and a shed, located just south of the station, housed No.2283 OLD BLUE for most of its operational life from October 1930 until condemned in September 1941. A G5 took over from thereon but the shed was closed in 1954. The station dated from February 1854 and was commissioned by the Middlesbrough & Guisborough Railway. Just one platform was provided with a bay on the right (overgrown by now) but the overall roof gave it some importance, at least in the eye of the owners. The bay on the left housed the goods shed. The whole building was demolished after closure. *K.H.Cockerill (ARPT).*

(*below*) D355 has charge of an afternoon Malton to Whitby passenger working at Grosmont on 14th September 1964. *John Boyes (ARPT).*

(*above*) D355 heads off on the last six miles to Whitby on that evening in September 1964. This line is still open for passenger traffic but superpower/suburban stock combinations are no longer the norm. *John Boyes (ARPT)*.

(*below*) D6757 hauls a mixed freight through Saltburn West on 14th August 1964. That gantry has a wonderful array of signals giving access to Saltburn terminus, the engine shed, and the onward route to the south. *John Boyes (ARPT)*.

North Yorkshire had lots of surprises for the visitor, not least the railway enthusiast. For a start there was the coastal industrial sprawl eastwards from the Tees round to Redcar on the east coast; however, travel a little further south and the Skinningrove steel complex, perched on the top of the sea cliffs, came into view. That particular works, complete with blast furnaces and all the various processes associated with changing iron-ore into finished steel is partly seen here in the left background on 2nd January 1969. The main part of the works was located to the right and behind the photographer. Along with the line from Loftus to Carlin How, Crag Hall signal box also looked after the sidings in the picture where Thornaby Type 3 D6829 is poised for some shunting. The steel industry around these parts was in decline and by 1970 many of the signal boxes has been closed. Crag Hall was one of them. No.6829 had recently lost its prefix but it was a newcomer to Thornaby having arrived from Gateshead in the previous December. It wasn't however its first stint at 51L having transferred there from Healey Mills in October 1966 but it then left for the first of two residencies at 52A. Having started life at Cardiff Canton in March 1963, the Co-Co was amongst the large batch of Type 3s which transferred en masse from South Wales to Healey Mills and York during the summer of 1966. *John Boyes (ARPT).*

Whit Monday 1964 in Scarborough was busy as usual and local motive power was represented by Swindon-built 0-6-0DM D.2151, the full point being peculiar to the Swindon built examples; Doncaster didn't bother. This dirty little urchin belonged to York shed and was out-stationed to Scarborough for the season. *John Boyes (ARPT).*

(*above*) 'Peak' D58 departs Scarborough with a London working – the old *FLYER*? – Sunday 5th August 1962. *N.W.Skinner (ARPT)*.

(*below*) Like D.2151, blue-liveried D2062 was photographed near Falsgrave signal box whilst working as one of the pilots at Scarborough (Londesborough Road) station. Some four years on – it is 6th April 1968 now – this 0-6-0DM is wearing the corporate blue livery with double arrows and managing to keep the prefix although it would be August at the earliest before those 'D's' started to disappear. The stock was from a Birmingham-Scarborough special. *John Boyes (ARPT)*.

Delivered from Vulcan Foundry during early July 1960, EE Type 4 D284 was still looking pristine when working an Up passenger train through Scarborough Mere on Saturday 30th of the month. Based initially at York, the big diesel remained at 50A for seven years before moving on to Gateshead. BR got twenty-three years of work from D284 and it was withdrawn from Healey Mills TMD in May 1983. *N.W.Skinner (ARPT)*.

Tinsley EE Type 3 D6808 departs from Bridlington on Monday 3rd June 1963. Although there is some superficial damage to the bodywork at the right front, the locomotive still has a hint of newness about it. *N.W.Skinner (ARPT)*.

EE Type 4 D259 in charge of the 1600 Malton to Whitby at Malton station on a rather cold 4th March 1965 – nice to see that steam heating working. The route taken was via Rillington and Grosmont (over the NYM) to give a direct approach to Whitby – see also pages 58 and 59. Note the closed and semi-derelict engine shed on the extreme left of the image. *John Boyes (ARPT)*.

D6790 on a petroleum working through Selby station on Friday 23rd February 1968: By now block trains are becoming more important to BR but at the cost of local goods yards, and those mighty marshalling yards of which some have barely been fully utilised and were soon to close! *R.F.Payne (ARPT)*.

One of York's own: EE Type 4 D258 on the 1456 departure to Colchester on 16th February 1962. *John Boyes (ARPT)*.

Two more of York's finest: Peppercorn K1 No.62047 heads a passenger working whilst south end station pilot BR Swindon-built 0-6-0DM D.2159 shunts a horsebox. The date is 6th June 1964 (just twenty years after D-Day!) when shed plates were still popular with the relevant authorities and fairly secure too. *John Boyes (ARPT)*.

Remember D2062 at Scarborough? Here she is on 1st November 1963 at the south end of York station. If she had been dumped on a siding you would immediately think that the shunter had been withdrawn. However, the fact that a Driver is there in the cab and the surrounding platforms, not to mention the permanent way, are quite dirty lets this urchin blend in somewhat. This Doncaster built 0-6-0DM (July 1959) became 03062 under TOPS and worked until June 1976 when she was purchased for preservation. *R.F.Payne (ARPT).*

By comparison, here is Finsbury Park's D9001 ST PADDY ticking-over in platform 14 on Saturday 6th October 1962 with a Down working – 1A22. Already more than a year old, this 'Deltic' would be one of the first two to be withdrawn – the other was D9020 NIMBUS, another 34G charge – in January 1980. Both were cut up at Doncaster shortly afterwards. Okay D9001, the clock is ticking! *John Boyes (ARPT).*

D9002 prior to its official naming ceremony at York station on 4th April 1963! *John Boyes (ARPT)*.

Named by the Regiment's Colonel-in-Chief, THE KING'S OWN YORKSHIRE LIGHT INFANTRY – which abbreviated nicely to KOYLI – D9002 has joined the growing band of 'namers' within the class. *John Boyes (ARPT)*.

We're back on platform 14 with D9002, which is also hauling 1A22 on this Thursday. 'What's all the fuss then?' *John Boyes (ARPT)*.

After its 15 minutes of fame, KOYLI starts to earn a living once again as that deafening 'Deltic' roar sweeps across the north end of York station. Take a good look at this image because you won't see too many 52A locomotives looking like this too often! *John Boyes (ARPT)*.

Lots of detail! D9001 in platform 14, again – 6th October 1962. *John Boyes (ARPT).*

This steam/diesel combination was recorded at York on 1st September 1962 when Brush Type 3 D5835 from Sheffield Darnall depot was coupled to Gresley V2 No.60935 to haul a southbound express. Delivered to 41A at the end of April 1962, D5835 had already spent six weeks on loan to Finsbury Park and was destined to head south again on 19th September with a transfer to Stratford. The V2 was one of Doncaster's fleet which had less than a year of operational life left before being condemned and then broken up. *N.W.Skinner (ARPT).*

I don't quite know what to make of this formation. This is Holgate platform on 1st June 1963 with one of York's recently acquired – from Gateshead on 27th February – BR Sulzer Type 2s D5099. The stock is all Southern Region and is nicely balanced with what looks like a buffet car in the set. Now was this train comprised eight new vehicles ex-York Carriage works? And were they for the SR? Was it third-rail electric stock or locomotive-hauled? York's 1963 output comprised eleven vehicles for the Liverpool Street–Clacton stock but they were a different colour. Perhaps this lot had been refurbished? Once again, if you know the answer then please contact the Publisher via the usual channels. *N.W.Skinner (ARPT).*

One of York's own batch of Brush Type 4s (D1100–D1111), D1101, waits at platform 15 with an Anglo-Scottish express shortly after delivery from Crewe in late August 1966. All twelve of this 'last Crewe-built batch' were initially allocated to York, its first examples of the 512-strong class. It was virtually four years to the day that the first Brush 4 – D1500 – was allocated to Finsbury Park depot (although it was doing-the-rounds of the LMR and WR at first). Since then the Loughborough factory of Brush and the BR locomotive works at Crewe had turned out that amazing number between them. Our subject became 47518 under Tops and was withdrawn in 1991 after an unknown but no doubt terrific mileage; or was it engine hours then? This class, even after their various problems in service, have given BR superb service and whoever took the plunge to eventually order such huge numbers of them had some nous. Note the point motor box alongside our subject. *Gordon Turner /GD/(ARPT).*

D9009 ALYCIDON runs through Doncaster on the Up fast with an Anglo-Scottish express circa 1966. An EE Type 3 heads north with a mixed freight whilst a Clayton Type 1 is returning to its home depot after a visit to shops. Note also the J50 works shunter which was still busy. Change had been taking place here for some years now and further developments were about to occur. There is no longer a main-line pilot for instance; all the trains are now diesel hauled and the requirement for such luxuries as having a main-line locomotive on stand-by for nearly 24-hours of every day appeared somewhat extravagant, wasteful perhaps? *A.R. Thompson coll. (ARPT).*

DONCASTER

We arrive at Doncaster just as D9008 THE GREEN HOWARDS roars through on the Down fast during the late morning of 3rd August 1964. The 'Deltic's' train is the *ANGLO SCOTTISH CAR CARRIER* which was made up of the usual load of four passenger vehicles including a buffet car and six car transporters. Note that all the engine room windows on D9008 are drawn open. Our own motive power from York was another 'Deltic' but we failed to record its number! *John Boyes (ARPT)*.

Tucked away in one of the south end bay platforms on the up side of Doncaster station was D9003 which became MELD in July 1961. Delivered from Newton-le-Willows to BR in March 1961, this 'Deltic' was one of the 34G Finsbury Park lot and in this illustration D9003 carries no shed plate so was probably still carrying out its acceptance trials which would date the image to circa April 1961, there being little or no dirt on any part of the locomotive. *Ian W. Coulson (ARPT)*.

The daily Uddingston-Cliffe cement empties heads south through a rather quiet Doncaster station on an unknown date circa 1963. The motive power is Hither Green BRC&W Type 3 D6562 which collected the train from an EE Type 4 at York, the northern limit to which these Southern Region locomotives worked on this particular duty. Yet to acquire a yellow warning panel, the Bo-Bo is in original ex-factory livery. *A.R. Thompson coll. (ARPT).*

Whilst we are in Doncaster a quick visit to the Plant works would not go amiss. This nice low winter sun image was captured on Sunday 4th January 1970 and features British Thompson-Houston Type 1 D8220, one of Stratford's 'finest' which has called in for some repair which High Meads couldn't (wouldn't) handle. Thirty-four of the forty-four strong class were built by Clayton Equipment Co. whilst the other ten were put together by the Yorkshire Engine Co. It made no difference as far as BR was concerned because the whole class were withdrawn during the period 1968 to 1972. Our subject got its marching orders in March 1971 and ended up at the BR locomotive works in Crewe and was broken up there in November; some twenty-five of the class met their end at Crewe. *R.Holland*

It wasn't all doom and gloom at Doncaster during those transition years when new diesel locomotives were turning up from the manufacturers every week. This North British Locomotive Co. Type 2 – D6123 – looks every bit the future but luckily nobody had the looking glass into the future so everything was rosy, at first. The date is 27th September 1959, a Sunday, and already Doncaster has received dozens of new diesels for acceptance trials. D6123 arrived from Glasgow on the previous Wednesday and was allocated to Ipswich depot once given the all-clear. After eight months at Ipswich the diesel-electric Bo-Bo was transferred to Eastfield in Glasgow; during that summer of 1960 all of the ER's NBL Type 2s were sent to Scotland – good riddance! *N.W. Skinner (ARPT)*.

Now here is Brush Type 2 D5550 on the same day – the AIA-AIA appears behind D6123 in the above image. However, that's where the similarity ends, sort of, because this Brush which arrived in Plant on Thursday was also destined to have Ipswich as its first depot. After that connection no further similarity exists; the Brush went on to serve BR reliably for many years until withdrawn in May 1995 as 31132 at Bescot. However, the 31 was not actually cut up until 2003 and then at the T.J. Thomson scrapyard in Stockton. The NBL Bo-Bo, after a period of alarming unreliability – along with the rest of the class – was chosen as the first of twenty to be refurbished. In June 1963 the original 1,000 h.p. engine was replaced with a more powerful Paxman Ventura engine of 1350 h.p. at the Davey Paxman works in Colchester. Did the change make any difference? D6123 along with the rest of the class were all scrapped by the end of 1972 except for one example – D6122 – which had been kept back by a certain scrapyard in South Wales in the hope that some group would come along and purchase the hulk for a lot more than the yard had paid for it. There being no takers, D6122 was broken up in 1980. Also in the Paint shop yard at Doncaster on this Sunday were EE Type 4 D234 (for the LMR and which had arrived Friday), and a BRC&W Type 2. *N.W. Skinner (ARPT)*.

(top) 'Baby Deltic' D5901 at Doncaster works on 24th April 1965 after arrival from Vulcan Foundry with newly built Type 3 D6977. D5901 was one of the class of ten which had everything going wrong for them from their initial arrival on BR in 1959 until finally being condemned. Much has been written about this small but nevertheless interesting group of locomotives and here we show its appearance at Doncaster after its refurbishment and then acceptance trials which in the case of this member was its third lot! *John Boyes (ARPT)*. *(centre & bottom)* Paint shop yard Sunday 16th July 1961: EE Type 5 D9008 and EE Type 4 D353 came from the same factory in Lancashire but arrived in Doncaster separately, D9008 came on Friday (the traditional day for Vulcan Foundry built locomotives to travel) 7th July whereas D353 came on Wednesday 12th July. The 'Deltic' was already a week into its acceptance trials and would be going to Gateshead a few days after this photograph was recorded. D353 was destined for York shed but it had a few more days of testing yet. Note the Brush Type 2 D5806 just getting into the frame. They were still arriving thick and fast from Loughborough. *N.W. Skinner (ARPT)*.

The destruction at the end of the line! This is, and you are going to have to take our word for it, No.15004, a Brush/LNER collaboration dating from September 1947 which managed to serve BR for just over twelve years before its non-standard design caught up with it. Initially allocated to March depot, the 0-6-0 diesel-electric shunter ended-up at New England shed and on a visit to Doncaster works, it was condemned on 5th October 1962. This is the unfortunate one-off in the 'Plant' scrapyard on 7th April 1963 with A4 60014 SILVER LINK for company. *N.W.Skinner (ARPT).*

'Baby Deltic' woes at Doncaster on 4th May 1969: Withdrawn D5907 and D5906 have been dumped by the side of the Crimpsall shops prior to their sale to a Kettering scrapyard where they met their end in July. There are more images of this unfortunate class illustrated later; hopefully we can shed a little more light on their somewhat premature demise. *R.Holland*

For those of you old enough to remember when such antics illustrated here were left to the discretion and awareness of the user, this image will bring back memories of another age where people, especially adults, were expected to behave responsibly and in doing so not endanger themselves or anyone else! But that's now ancient history like the days when invading Vikings could pillage all before them. That 1960s history might as well be a thousand years ago but it was only 12th September 1964 when this lot of former Vikings debated the events of the day and the forthcoming attractions courtesy of BR. The location is of course Skeggy and it's about lunchtime. One foolhardy enthusiast has removed his jacket but he is at least looking and listening for the next arrival as he crosses the track! So, what are the details of this image? The Brush 4 was D1564 from Immingham depot; the Stanier Cl.5 was Nottingham based No.44851 heading what appears to be the second train of the *BLIDWORTH WELFARE CHILDENS OUTING*. The atrocious external condition probably did little to endear BR to the miners who organised this trip. The B1 is No.61188 from Colwick which may have been the engine heading the No.1 Blidworth special but Skegness was a popular destination for weekends away from Nottingham anyway. *John Boyes (ARPT).*

On a quiet Wednesday 15th July 1964, 204 h.p. 0-6-0DM shunter D2299 earning its keep as station pilot at Lincoln (Central). Lincoln cathedral stands high above the city watching the expansion and change as it has done for hundreds of years. Did you know the cathedral was once the tallest building in the world, a spire on the central tower gave it a height of 525ft.; that was until a storm in 1549 caused it to collapse! Work on the building started in 1072 and continued until 1311. Thanks to the wool trade Lincoln became England's third largest city by the 13th century, after London and York; we're covering all those places in this tome. *John Boyes (ARPT).*

(*above*) Skirting across Lincolnshire now to its western boundary we arrive at Stamford, another ancient cross-roads with much history under its belt. On 25th June 1964 one of Leicester's BRC&W Type 2s, D5387, runs through Stamford (Town) station with a westbound freight. Note the beautifully tended garden plot on the opposite platform. *John Boyes (ARPT)*.

(*below*) A passenger working from Stamford (Town) to Leicester (London Road) on that June day in 1964; the train originated at Peterborough (East) as the 1210 departure, and the motive power was this Cricklewood based Type 2 D7577. Steam – looks like an Ivatt Cl.4 – is shunting the sidings in the distance whilst another rather smartly tended garden patch takes our eye at the platform end. *John Boyes (ARPT)*.

The very same BR Sulzer Type 2 and its Leicester train in platform 6 at Peterborough (North) on that 26th June. Time to step aboard Mr Boyes! *John Boyes (ARPT)*.

Before the arrival of the Leicester train, there was a busy moment at Peterborough (North) as 'Deltic D9017 DURHAM LIGHT INFANTRY is pegged for the north just as Finsbury Park Brush Type 4 D1511 runs in with an Up express on that Friday in June 1964. *John Boyes (ARPT)*.

Passing New England yards and engine shed (much of which was blocked out of view by Brush D1503 and its stationery train) on the Leicester service, John Boyes bagged this Finsbury Park urchin on film as a secondary objective. *John Boyes (ARPT).*

Peterborough (East) station pilot on 26th June 1964 was 0-6-0DM D2222 which was one of the March allocation. Originally numbered 11128, this shunter was renumbered in 1960; it transferred to Gateshead on 14th July 1968 but by November it was withdrawn; after spending months stored inside Heaton shed, the little diesel ended up in a Rotherham scrapyard during the summer of 1969. The background to our subject locomotive is formed by the erstwhile Great Eastern engine shed which was operational until April 1939 when the LNER closed it and concentrated all their motive power matters in Peterborough at New England. The building is now apparently listed! *John Boyes (ARPT).*

(*above*) Between the two Welwyn tunnels, Brush D5611 hauls a blue-liveried set of commuter stock on an outer suburban service during the summer of 1970. *M.F. Best (ARPT)*.

(*below*) The mainstay of the King's Cross suburban services for many years, the Brush Type 2s certainly proved their worth with the motive power authorities. Finsbury Park depot had dozens of them allocated but at any one time they would be scattered the length and breadth of the ECML as far north as Hitchin. On Monday 10th October 1966 D5598 has charge of a Down working from the Widened lines. This Type 2 was new to Hornsey in March 1960 but on the 24th of the following month relocated to the newly opened Finsbury Park (34G). A year later on 24th March 1961 it transferred to Stratford – such 'local' moves were commonplace between the two principal ER London depots – but returned to 34G on 24th July 1965. *R.F. Payne (ARPT)*.

Now for a few pages of serious 'Deltic' nostalgia, at 'The Cross' – Haymarket's D9000 ROYAL SCOTS GREY departs on a rather dull Sunday 5th April 1964. The signal box had recently undergone a repaint to its exterior surfaces whilst someone has left two gas bottles on a trolley by the boarded crossing; nowadays such a trivial event would see the station evacuated, trains stopped at Hornsey, and the bomb squad called. I never realised the platform ramp there was built from timber! *John Boyes (ARPT)*.

Remember D9020 at Newcastle on page 8? Well, this is that same train about to be sent off from 'The Cross' by well-wishers! *H.C. Robinson (ARPT)*.

D9020 again but on 24th May 1965 on 1A54, the 1805hrs Newcastle service. The deplorable state of King's Cross station is apparent in this image if you look at the screens of the train shed where both glass windows and timber cladding are missing. *A.R. Thompson coll. (ARPT).*

Haymarket's D9004 QUEEN'S OWN HIGHLANDER on the *FLYING SCOTSMAN* and displaying that 'flying thistle' headboard which was a short-lived innovation (1963 to 68'?). Although we have no date for this 1960s scene, it's near 1000hrs and the station is recovering from the rush-hour arrivals with Brush Type 2s making ready with empty stock for Holloway and beyond. *A.R. Thompson coll. (ARPT).*

The 1960s were interesting times from a motive power point of view; this diesel for instance was one of those ‘try-it-and-see’ jobs from Brush. Numbered D0280 and named FALCON, the Eastern Region had the first ‘go’ of it and here it is on 16th August 1962 running out of the station en route to the stabling point. D0280 had been received by the ER during the previous October and it was allocated to Finsbury Park. BR actually purchased the locomotive in December 1970 by which time it was working on the Western Region. However it was stored in May 1974 as non-standard and then in October 1975 it was withdrawn followed by the inevitable sale to a scrapyard. It was cut up in March 1976. *D.J. Dippie*.

Assuming D5900 is working empty stock in and out of the terminus, this interesting composition from circa 1968 reveals one of the Officers saloons tagged onto what will become the rear of a Pullman train; the full brake must have been the ‘buffer’ between the customers and the BR personnel. The grubby ‘Baby Deltic’ was withdrawn by the end of the year. *M.F.Best (ARPT)*.

Oh we are not finished with the 'Deltic's' yet! On yet another morning express, D9004 gets away via Main 2 whilst the station ticks over nicely during its morning routine. *A.R. Thompson coll. (ARPT).*

'Deltics,' everywhere! Five of them grace 'Bottom Shed' locomotive yard at King's Cross station circa 1963 with D9001 and D9021 identified whilst the other three tick-over in the corner. This was probably the winter of 1962-63 when even London had some snow. D9021 was not named until November 1963 and the old steam locomotive coaling plant is still in situ, and those front warning panels have got bigger! *Frank Bell (ARPT).*

The forty-four BTH Type 1s introduced over a four year period from 1957 to 1961 were initially distributed with ten of them working on the LM Region from Devons Road shed, and the rest scattered about the Eastern Region from March (actually sub-shedded at King's Lynn) to Stratford and Finsbury Park to Ipswich and Norwich. By 1966 those which were not already allocated to 30A were all starting to migrate to Stratford. In 1968 when withdrawals started they were all in east London. This is D8234 at Liverpool Street on 16th February 1969 at the head of a parcels train. By now half of the class were either withdrawn or laid-up. In March 1971 the rest of the class, active or not, were condemned. Many were sent to Crewe for breaking up whereas others went to private scrapyards. Note the real Mini on the platform. *Chris Campbell.*

Stratford Freightliner terminal Monday 22nd April 1968! The inaugural service of the London to Paris Freightliner is about to depart and sent off with some ceremony whilst one of Stratford's own Brush 4s, D1758 heads the train. Of course there was no Chunnel then, nor were we members of the EU but the French Ambassador turned out as did the Chairman of BR. Note the seasonal showers. Some things never change! *W.R.E. Lewis (ARPT).*

(*above*) To start off our depot sequence let's look at the second – in numerical order – 'Baby Deltic' stabled on the shed yard at Hornsey circa May 1959. We are assuming that D5901 had by now been accepted by BR and the weight issues have been dealt with and the Bo-Bo is ready for work. The first thing to notice – actually there are two things so we'll start at the front – is the wrap-around bufferbeam red paint which has also been taken up onto the bodywork and ends in line with the second glaring item, the white cheat-line running the whole length of the lower body!! Whoever thought of that one didn't know much about railway vehicles, or indeed any vehicles! I nearly forgot the roof but a few diesel locomotives were treated to such, short-sightedness! I must admit that the image certainly catches the eye and the whole scene looks a bit, bizarre? We'll be seeing more of these diesels in the coming pages. *Les Waters coll.*

(*below*) Same depot, Hornsey, but now with steam safely out of the way and with the establishment titled Traction Maintenance Depot. This is D5905 – told you we'd be seeing more of them – stabled alongside the shed on 29th June 1969. Of course, this is the rebuilt version with two-tone green livery, a lighter green replacing that white band illustrated so eloquently above. D5905 is still in traffic at this time and would be for another eighteen months to become the penultimate Class 23 standing after younger sister D5909. Some of the class had already gone indeed whilst this image was being recorded five of the class were being taken apart in Kettering. Note the 34G which was a painted-on version of the shed plate. *R.Holland*

The forty-four BTH Type 1s introduced over a four year period from 1957 to 1961 were initially distributed with ten of them working on the LM Region from Devons Road shed, and the rest scattered about the Eastern Region from March (actually sub-shedded at King's Lynn) to Stratford and Finsbury Park to Ipswich and Norwich. By 1966 those which were not already allocated to 30A were all starting to migrate to Stratford. In 1968 when withdrawals started they were all in east London. This is D8234 at Liverpool Street on 16th February 1969 at the head of a parcels train. By now half of the class were either withdrawn or laid-up. In March 1971 the rest of the class, active or not, were condemned. Many were sent to Crewe for breaking up whereas others went to private scrapyards. Note the real Mini on the platform. *Chris Campbell.*

Stratford Freightliner terminal Monday 22nd April 1968! The inaugural service of the London to Paris Freightliner is about to depart and sent off with some ceremony whilst one of Stratford's own Brush 4s, D1758 heads the train. Of course there was no Chunnel then, nor were we members of the EU but the French Ambassador turned out as did the Chairman of BR. Note the seasonal showers. Some things never change! *W.R.E. Lewis (ARPT).*

(*above*) To start off our depot sequence let's look at the second – in numerical order – 'Baby Deltic' stabled on the shed yard at Hornsey circa May 1959. We are assuming that D5901 had by now been accepted by BR and the weight issues have been dealt with and the Bo-Bo is ready for work. The first thing to notice – actually there are two things so we'll start at the front – is the wrap-around bufferbeam red paint which has also been taken up onto the bodywork and ends in line with the second glaring item, the white cheat-line running the whole length of the lower body!! Whoever thought of that one didn't know much about railway vehicles, or indeed any vehicles! I nearly forgot the roof but a few diesel locomotives were treated to such, short-sightedness! I must admit that the image certainly catches the eye and the whole scene looks a bit, bizarre? We'll be seeing more of these diesels in the coming pages. *Les Waters coll.*

(*below*) Same depot, Hornsey, but now with steam safely out of the way and with the establishment titled Traction Maintenance Depot. This is D5905 – told you we'd be seeing more of them – stabled alongside the shed on 29th June 1969. Of course, this is the rebuilt version with two-tone green livery, a lighter green replacing that white band illustrated so eloquently above. D5905 is still in traffic at this time and would be for another eighteen months to become the penultimate Class 23 standing after younger sister D5909. Some of the class had already gone indeed whilst this image was being recorded five of the class were being taken apart in Kettering. Note the 34G which was a painted-on version of the shed plate. *R.Holland*

Over to Stratford now and we are beginning to see some settling snow and frozen locomotives. *(top)* BTH Type 1 D8223 heads a line of withdrawn locomotives at Stratford on 16th February 1969; shunter D3445 is behind. In case you've forgotten the notice on the wall reads 'Notice. It is strictly forbidden to ride cycles about the premises.' *(centre)* The snow is falling now as our photographer tries to record these images: D2223 in full and final livery. This shunter was transferred to Colchester before withdrawal in May 1971. *(bottom)* BTH Bo-Bo D8221 was still active and would remain so until February 1971. *All Chris Campbell.*

(*above*) Brush Type 2s and Stratford went hand-in-hand! If as an enthusiast you wanted to see this class then Stratford was the place to come and visit, especially on a Sunday. However, on Friday 17th August 1962 D5537 and classmate D5591 bask in the sunshine in the shed yard alongside one of the sheds erected specifically for diesel locomotive maintenance. *D.J.Dippie.*

(*below*) Ex-works BR Sulzer Type 2 D5064 must be the smartest of her class in this album. D5064 was photographed outside the High Meads shops at Stratford on 17th August 1962. *D.J.Dippie.*

(*above*) D5903 laid up at Stratford on 17th August 1962. This storage was during their first period of idleness when virtually all of the class ended-up alongside the High Mead shops whilst negotiations were in play to see what if anything could be done about them. Note that the white cheat-line has stood up to road dirt quite well over the three years since this locomotive was put into traffic although in reality D5903 and its sisters had done very little work anyway. *D.J.Dippie.*

(*below*) In 1969 Stratford depot became a dumping ground for many of its own allocation which had recently been withdrawn as either useless or non-standard. These two shunting locomotives – photographed on Sunday 8th June 1969 – fell into the latter group: the 0-6-0DE D3629 because it had a Blackstone engine and GEC traction motors as opposed to the standard 0-6-0DE with English Electric engine and motors. The 0-6-0DM D2215 would have become part of designated Class 04 had any of them lasted long enough but they too were different from their cousins which became Class 03. Basically the 03 had been built in the BR workshops of Doncaster and Swindon whilst the 04 had been built by private contractors – mainly Vulcan Foundry at Newton-le-Willows and the RSH factories at Darlington and Newcastle. The engines, the trusted Gardner 8L3, were the same, the mechanical transmission, gearbox, and the final drive also. They were all of Drewry design! Over the ten years of production some design changes took place, some subtle, some not so subtle. The exhaust stack was one of those details with a number of variations carried (our subject has the traffic cone, probably the least attractive of the lot). The cab was another area where changes took place over time but basically these 30-ton shunters were very useful and reliable servants. All of the 04s had gone by May 1972 but 1968 was the worst year for their withdrawals with most of those going for scrap; it was only afterwards that their usefulness in private industry was realised by which time most had become the proverbial razor blades. D2215 had been withdrawn in February 1969 but ten years were to pass before it was scrapped in Long Marston, whilst D3629 had succumbed in May. *R. Holland.*

(top) End of the line for withdrawn BTH D8243 at Stratford on 8th June 1969? Not quite because this, the last of the class built, was eventually taken into Departmental Stock as 968000. *(centre)* Lighting never strikes twice! Or does it? BTH D8237 was just in front of D8243 and she too was taken into Departmental Stock as 968002. So, which one became 968001 – why D8233 of course! *Both R.Holland.* *(bottom)* The prototype Deltic visiting Stratford – 11th March 1960! *R.F.Payne (ARPT).*

This is Gateshead – honest! Only those of you who had visited the depot knew about this washing machine and most of you thought it was broken! The image of D1572 passing through the appliance on 17th April 1971 was captured by a local photographer. *Dave Tyreman (ARPT)*.

Thornaby's D6761 and sister D6762 with a DBT rest for the weekend alongside the old coaling stage at West Hartlepool engine shed after steam had moved out – actually vacated the region – in September 1967. *Gordon Turner/GD/ (ARPT)*.

One for the modellers: Front end detail on a fairly new D1515 at Neville Hill depot on Sunday 5th May 1963. Put into traffic on 29th March 1963 and allocated to Finsbury Park, this Brush was sent on loan to Neville Hill on 10th April; it left Leeds and headed back to 34G on 12th June. *John Boyes (ARPT)*.

Becoming part of the Eastern Region in February 1958, the former Midland Railway engine shed at Grimesthorpe, Sheffield was coded 41B under Darnall. The depot comprised a square roundhouse and an outside 65ft diameter turntable with stabling roads radiating around its western perimeter. As Darnall 41A began to receive new diesel locomotives of all shapes and sizes, it soon ran out of room so the spare stabling space at Grimesthorpe was utilised, especially the outside turntable for the growing fleet of main-line diesels. This image captured on Sunday 7th May, 1961 during an enthusiasts visit, reveals Brush Type 2 D5685 stabled on one of the turntable roads. Steam was still allocated to 41B and a WD 2-8-0 can be seen in the middle background but their days were numbered at this depot and they were evicted on 11th September leaving the facility for that expanding pool of diesel locomotives. D5685 had been delivered new to Sheffield – part of a batch of fifteen – in February but in those days it didn't take long for new to look used! The next batch of fifty-nine Brush Type 2s destined for Sheffield was in the making with the first of them arriving any day soon. These were followed by a similar number of EE Type 3s, Brush Type 4s, and vast numbers of 350 h.p. 0-6-0DE shunters; it was getting crowded around Sheffield but a new purpose built depot was being created to look after this fleet. Grimesthorpe's out-dated shed building and the coaling plant were demolished whilst the diesels continued to stable until 1964 when Tinsley was opened. *N.W.Skinner (ARPT).*

Awaiting delivery to Bradford's Hammerton Street diesel depot, new BR Doncaster-built Drewry 204 h.p. 0-6-0DMs D2089 and D2090 outside the repair shop at Doncaster Carr motive power depot on 8th May 1960. This engine shed, even at this time, was full of contrasts with the likes of these new locomotives rubbing shoulders with Gresley and Peppercorn Pacifics which were awaiting overhaul or were ex-shops looking as smart as this pair. *N.W.Skinner (ARPT).*

The east end of Thornaby's straight shed on the evening of Wednesday 27th May 1964 with an array of resident English Electric Type 3s – D6773, D6774, and D6768 identified, a Type 4 – D397, a couple of BR Sulzer Type 2s – D5164 and D5154, and a single unidentified BRC&W Type 2. The water gantry has all but been moth-balled whereas the problematic overhead sanding gantry was on the point of being temporary decommissioned. As usual BR cheap-skated when this depot was built and instead of installing tried, tested and proven North American-type equipment, they went for a cheaper and untried alternative! *John Boyes (ARPT).*

(*above*) Three years on and looking across the east end of Thornaby's straight shed again but south to north this time on Thursday 17th August 1967. Visiting Peppercorn K1 No.62005 has come on shed but there is no water gantry note whilst the sanding equipment has been somewhat altered, refurbished and was hopefully working. DBT No.B964072 is awaiting entry for servicing whilst one of 51L's EE Type 1s remains inconspicuous. Besides generating a bit of smoke, the K1 has raised some interest too, steam being all but banished from this depot. However, it got there somehow from its then home shed at Tyne Dock in order to work a special up the Wensleydale branch amongst others on the following Sunday; in the meantime it was cleaned up for the event. No.62005 was transferred to Holbeck on 10th September and withdrawn on the penultimate day of 1967. Of course, it is now well and truly preserved. *John Boyes (ARPT)*.

(*below*) As can be seen from this image captured on 19th July 1969, Thornaby's Clayton fleet were looking somewhat jaded. This is D8601 and sister apparently coupled to the depot's breakdown train. At this time this particular Type 1 was less than five years old. It was soon to move on to Scotland where most of the class ended their days; hopefully a wash might have taken place prior to transfer but the odds were slim! D8601 ended its time in October 1971 at Haymarket depot. It was broken up at Glasgow works in 1973. *Sam Woods*

Built for steam and now largely useless! A section of the roundhouse at Thornaby on 27th May 1964 is given over to the Drewry 0-6-0DMs allocated to 51L. D2320 on the left is with a stores van whilst an unidentified member is stabled with a stored DBT which weighed more than the 0-6-0. The 70ft diameter turntable serving this facility was never going to be worn out, since its opening it had hardly been worked to its full capacity and as far as this compiler can remember the stalls in this building had never been fully utilised. *John Boyes (ARPT)*.

Two 'namers' grace York shed yard on Friday 26th June 1964: BR Sulzer Type 4 D58 THE KING'S OWN ROYAL BORDER REGIMENT from Derby, and 'Jubilee' No.45623 PALESTINE from Newton Heath. Both locomotives are dirty, one considerably so but that didn't seem to matter because the Manchester engine was withdrawn a month later being condemned during the week ending 25th July. *John Boyes (ARPT)*.

Livery transition period 10th August 1968! Two 'Peaks' D132 (Nottingham Division) and D167 (Holbeck), and a Tinsley based Brush, D1788, stable for the weekend at York. York motive power depot had always been a meeting place for lots of visiting locomotives but during the diesel era it became even more cosmopolitan with more locomotives from other regions. These three were regarded as virtually 'locals' in the great scheme of things whereas in other parts of the yard visitors from Bristol, Cardiff, March, Stratford, Haymarket, Aberdeen, Eastfield and Crewe could be found. York's own allocation of main-line diesel locomotives diminished over the years as traffic patterns changed and indeed multiple units became more popular. At the end of 1967 summer timetable the main-line locomotive allocation at York – now coded 55B – was seventeen English Electric Type 4s, eleven Brush Type 4s, a pair of BR Sulzer Type 2s, and ten EE Type 1s, along with numerous shunting locomotives of 204 h.p. and 350 h.p. types. Steam by now did not exist in York although pockets could still be found in other centres. *J. Archer (ARPT).*

The north end of York engine shed yard on Monday 28th June 1965 with some surprising visitors which had been stabled for an unknown period. Tinsley's brand-new Brush 4 D1870 heads the line-up which also includes new, but not yet taken into traffic, AL6 E3115. Bringing up the rear with a brake van attached is a grubby, and more than two years old, AL5 E3088. On the previous Saturday both of the electrics had been stabled inside the steam locomotive shed at Darlington so we can assume they were brought south at any time from Saturday evening up to this Monday morning. However, and more to the point, what were the pair doing at Darlington anyway? The answer lay with the turntable located at the south end of Darlington (Bank Top) passenger station on the Down side where, during the previous week, both of these locomotives – it's not known if the Brush 4 was involved too – went through 'Torsion Tests' whereby one bogie was run onto the turntable whilst the other remained on the fixed rails. The table' was then gradually turned and measurements were taken. These were not the first a.c. electric locomotives to undergo testing on the Darlington table' because some weeks earlier AL5 E3068 and Vulcan Foundry-built AL6 E3174 (another latecomer to the 'in-traffic' club) had attended – interesting times indeed! Both electric locomotives were Doncaster built, and E3088 was the first of its class to be withdrawn in July 1984 as 85033. *Dave Tyreman (ARPT).*

A rose between two thorns!? New Brush Type 4 D1576 stables on York shed yard on 1st Sept 1963. One of the thorns was D390 whilst the identity of the other is unknown. The Brush was on a delivery run to Gateshead and it looks as though York has waylaid it as was always the way with 50A. New stuff going north on delivery: use it; ex-works stuff going south from Darlington; use it. It is a wonder anything ever got past York. Oh yes, I take back what I said at the bottom of page 67. *Ian W. Coulson (ARPT).*

We've already seen one of the LNER's 0-6-0DE shunters in dire straits at Doncaster. This is another of that small band of pioneering diesel shunters which also went on to serve BR for many years. We have no date for this image captured at March depot fairly late in the day but 15002 – just look at those solid wheels – was sent on loan to the LM Region on 9th January 1966 and to Crewe South depot permanently from 30th January. She was condemned on 5th August 1967 and sold for scrap. *K.H. Cockerill (ARPT).*

Whoops! They've started! First it was blue paint, now the 'D' prefix was disappearing. And look, no shedplate just two bolts doing nothing! What does that transfer say? Which one, large or small? Small one has the shed name with the old code underneath; the larger transfer gives a load of information about the locomotive. Looks like it could do with a repaint in that corporate blue! (D)5664 at March circa 1970? *K.H.Cockerill (ARPT).*

(*below*) Hull Dairycoates circa 1967 when one of the wackiest mass transfers of BR diesel locomotives took place. It all started with weak management at the highest levels, stronger management at the intermediate levels, obstinacy, stupidity, waste and sheer pig-headedness! Around the outside turntable at the eastern end of the depot are four of the fifty-six former Western Region 0-6-0DH trip locomotives built at Swindon during 1964 and 1965. Firstly, they were all of the diesel-hydraulic type, of which the BRB had no further use as it had favoured diesel-electric traction. Of course the (Great) Western Region were the instigators of the diesel-hydraulic genre and they wanted their own way and so ordered dozens and dozens of the type to be work on their part of the system. However, the 0-6-0DH trip locomotives were already doomed before the first one was completed at Swindon in July 1964 (they actually pushed six into traffic that month just to make a point) but Swindon and its Regional management were going to have those fifty-odd locomotives no matter what. And so it came to pass that nobody knew what to do with them as soon as they were put into traffic. The economics were incredible, the waste scandalous but nobody was ever brought to book at any level of BR management. Needless to say the D95XX diesels were being put into store without having turned a wheel in revenue service. Some were soon to be scrapped! What to do next! Send them away to pastures far and wide. And so the first nineteen of those allocated to the North Eastern Region (it had become part of an expanded Eastern Region by then) arrived at Dairycoates in 1966, followed by another thirteen in 1967. The following year they had gone; mainly to the National Coal Board and British Steel, two – incidentally – state owned industries! The whole story of the Class 14s is a debacle from a further period of modern British history where madness ruled! *I.W. Coulson (ARPT).*

(top) I'm not sure if there was a name for this livery variation but I'm sure slow corrosion wouldn't go amiss! This is EE Type 3 D6791 at Dairycoates circa 1967. Notice anything different? That is correct it's got different ends from those it was built with. The locomotive had been involved in an accident at Ryhope Grange in 1966 which damaged the ends and the cabs. The resultant rebuilding saw this, the final variation carried by the class, with the central code boxes. Behind D6791 is one of its sisters, D6793 with the second front end variation with split boxes as originally worn by our subject. Now, about that complexion! *I.W. Coulson (ARPT)*. *(centre)* D6739 arrived at Dairycoates in 1962 with D6732 to D6736, D6738 to D6741, and D6779 to D6783. The date – 22nd April 1968, a Monday! *(bottom)* It must not be forgotten that Dairycoates was also home to six EE Type 1s – D8310 to D8315 – from 1968 until the wind-down of main-line traction in Hull in 1969. This is D8312 stabled on one of the outside turntable stalls on that Saturday in April 1968. *Both Dave Tyreman (ARPT)*.

Finsbury Park fuelling point on 8th June 1969 with *(top)* D8231 awaiting its turn. *(centre)* D8232 is close behind. *(bottom)* D5901 is still with us. *All R.Holland.*

As a sort of tribute to those useless 'Baby Deltics' we finish off our London area depots with this trilogy of laid-up members on that sunny Sunday in June 1969 with *(top)* D5903 withdrawn during the previous November *(centre)* D5900 also withdrawn previous November, and *(bottom)* D5904 which lasted until the previous January. All three were just days away from being hauled off to Kettering and oblivion! *All R. Holland.*

The diesel depot at Blyth Cambois (pronounced Cammus) was opened for business on 1st October 1967 and replaced the old steam roundhouse at North Blyth. *(left)* Although the weekend occupancy of 'Cammus' could be quite healthy, all of the motive power was supplied by Gateshead including the shunting locomotives such as D3243 sporting the BR double-arrow along with a 'D' prefix. *(above)* EE Type 1s D8019 and D8026 stabled for the weekend. These two Type 1s came from different builders and different years. D8019 was one of the original batch built by Vulcan Foundry for the LM Region in March 1958 and had oval buffers; D8026 came from RS&H in December 1959 and had round buffers. Both had been blessed with Gateshead's brand of filth. *(bottom)* D6797 was another which had acquired the double-arrow symbol and retained the 'D' prefix probably after shopping at Doncaster. The depot's closure in September 1994 coincided with the near total run-down of mining operations in the area. *All Chris Campbell.*

The stabling point at Tyne Yard is our last port of call and the top image shows the weekend line-up on Saturday 19th April 1969 with six Clayton Type 1s and an EE Type 3 alongside its larger Type 4 cousin, all basking in the spring sunshine. *(centre)* D8599 looking half decent – for a Clayton, from Gateshead – and which has had its end yellow warning panel refreshed. The Gateshead and Thornaby allocations of these unpredictable locomotives appeared to give less trouble than those at other depots but the reporting of incidents in the North-East was somewhat sketchy during the period when they worked there. *(bottom)* We don't have the number of the green Type 3 but the blue Type 4 is easy enough to spot in its Gateshead combination of filth, oil, road dirt (modellers note how subtle that is) over blue livery with yellow ends, and a black underframe. D237 had spent the whole of its nine years and six-month life so far working mainly from 52A and 51L. Everything you see on this page has now gone although that Type 3 could contradict that statement! *All Chris Campbell.*